Learning How To Avoid
The Gap

Canadian Cataloguing in Publication Data

Sullivan, Dan, 1944-
Learning how to avoid the gap: the skill of build-
ing lifetime happiness

ISBN 1-896635-17-2

1. Success in business. 2. Entrepreneurship –
Psychological aspects. 3. Happiness. I. Title

HF 5386.S94 1999   650.1   C99-931332-0

Printed in Toronto, Canada. March 2008. The Strategic Coach Inc., 33 Fraser Avenue, Suite 201, Toronto, Ontario, M6K 3J9.

This publication is meant to strengthen your common sense, not substitute for it. It is also not a substitute for the
advice of your doctor, lawyer, accountant, or any of your advisors, personal or professional.

If you would like further information about the Strategic Coach® Program or other Strategic Coach® services and products,
please telephone 416.531.7399 or 1.800.387.3206. Fax: 416.531.1135. Email: info@strategiccoach.com.

Learning How To Avoid The Gap™.

There are many people in this world who are enormously successful, live in wonderful circumstances, and have extraordinary opportunities. Yet they are unhappy — and it keeps getting worse. At the same time, there are others with all of these same achievements and advantages who are happy — increasingly so. Why the difference? Why are some successful people happy and others not? I believe it's because of the way people's brains work. The happy individuals look at life from one perspective; the unhappy look at life from another.

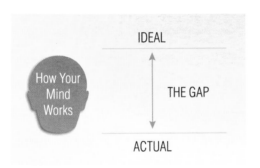

Three capabilities of the mind.

Our minds are very complex, and yet we can think about how they work in very simple terms. The diagram above illustrates three major capabilities of the human mind: "The Gap," the "Actuals," and the "Ideal." I define each of them on the following page.

3

The Gap: This is the permanent difference that exists between our Actuals and our Ideals.

The Actuals: These are our actual achievements and results in life — either external ones like income and wealth, or internal ones like learning.

The Ideal: This is a "mental construct" — a tool of our brain — that enables us to come to grips with the future. The Ideal is a picture that we create of future desirable events and situations that enables us to move forward in time. The Ideal does not actually exist outside of our minds, nor is it achievable. The Ideal has a number of powerful purposes. It enables us to:
- Establish goals.
- Motivate ourselves.
- Withstand hardships and difficulties.

The Gap, the Actuals, and the Ideal: In order to be both successful and happy in life, it's important to understand the proper use of these mental capabilities.

The Ideal and the horizon.
Our brains have many different kinds of "mental constructs."
Another one that is very much like the Ideal is called the
"horizon." When we walk outside and look ahead of us to
where the ground ends and the sky begins, there is a line
that is called the horizon. At a very early age, we learn the
horizon doesn't actually exist outside of our minds. We
accept, both intellectually and emotionally, that the horizon
is not reachable. It's simply a thinking tool that enables us to
come to grips with physical space.

Failure to learn about the Ideal.
The horizon analogy is very useful because it points out
the importance of understanding how our minds work.
Why is it that virtually everyone can accept the horizon as
just a mental construct, whereas many people have lifelong
difficulty in accepting the Ideal as just a thinking tool?

The most obvious answer is that we can see physical space
(horizon), but we cannot "see" future time (Ideal) in the
same way. Learning about the horizon comes naturally, but
learning about the Ideal often requires education, and
many human beings never receive it.

The source of unhappiness.
When successful individuals don't learn that the Ideal is just a mental construct — and that there is always a permanent "gap" between their actual achievements and the Ideal — the chances are very great that they will lead chronically unhappy lives. They will also make the lives of many other people around them unnecessarily difficult and frustrating in the process.

How your mind works.
Understanding the proper role of the Ideal is life's single most crucial lesson. Once this lesson is learned, it becomes possible to avoid forming a habit called "thinking in 'The Gap,'" which is the principal source of unhappiness for a great number of people — especially among those people who are the most talented, ambitious, and successful in all fields of activity.

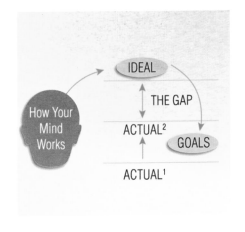

The Ideal creates goals.

The best way to look at your ideals is as an infinite source of inspiration for creating goals. We are all like movie makers, using our entire memory and imagination as raw material for casting a never-ending series of pictures out in front of us. We are doing this all the time. Otherwise, we couldn't even get out of bed in the morning. The moment we wake up, we begin using our ideals to create a unique picture of the day ahead. It is this picture that allows us to begin planning out our activities. What is most important in this process is that we begin to establish a series of goals that represent our achievements for the day.

Goals create two Actuals.

Goals are marvelous creations, and goal setting is a marvelous creative activity. There will never be any computer in the world that can match your brain's ability to identify and establish a goal. In a split second, billions of small decisions are made in your mind, and they establish something quite dramatic: two Actuals. First you identify an Actual[1], which is where you are right now. Then you immediately establish an Actual[2], which is where you want to be when you accomplish the goal. The moment you establish these two Actuals, you

are filled with a tremendous motivating energy to move forward. It's quite a remarkable phenomenon, and you do it
dozens of times every day.

Everyone's brain works this way.
Our brains all work in this goal-setting fashion. We all have
powerful ideals, we all create pictures in front of us, and all
of us are continually involved in the process of establishing
big and small goals — Actual[1] to Actual[2] — that motivate us
to take action. This is the way human brains operated ten
thousand years ago, the way they
operate today, and the way
brains will operate ten thousand
years from now.

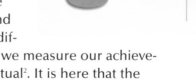

**The crucial question: How do you
measure Actual[2]?**
Although we are all alike in the
way we use our ideals to set and
pursue goals, we are radically dif-
ferent from each other in how we measure our achievement when we arrive at our Actual[2]. It is here that the
crucial issue of happiness comes into the picture, because

our ability to be happy in life hinges on the single question of how we measure our achievements. It is almost as if there were a measurement switch installed in everyone's brain. Depending on which way this switch is moved, people will either be happy or unhappy in their achievements. Relating this back to the mind diagram, the two ways of measuring are by the *Ideal* or by *Actual*[1].

The decision between an unhappy or happy life.
Our happiness depends on how we perform the act of measurement. We are always measuring one thing or another. It's probably the one brain activity that we do more than any other. We measure space. We measure time. We have created an infinite series of rules and standards that allows us to differentiate one experience from another, one thing from another. It's not too bold a statement to make that our very ability to think has come about because of our ability to measure things.

The smartest people are those with the best ability to measure one experience against another. At the same time, it's ironic that some of the smartest people are also the unhappiest people. This is because they have never

learned the proper way to measure the single most important thing in their daily lives — their achievements.

**Measuring by the Ideal leads to a sense of failure and
unhappiness.**
Because the Ideal is a mental construct — and therefore not
achievable — it makes no sense to use it as a measurement
of our achievements. Yet millions of people do, every single
day. The result is a continual sense of missing the mark. No
matter how great your achievements are, if you measure
against the Ideal, you will always come up short. You will
always feel deficient.

People who measure their Actual[2] against the Ideal have a per-
petual sense of failure throughout their lives. This is accompa-
nied by a sense of frustration. Every time they set a goal, they
expect to reach The Ideal, and these desires and aspirations
are always frustrated.

They feel like losers.
They have a sense of disappointment — with themselves,
with others, and with life itself. The resulting feeling over
the course of a lifetime is one of low self-esteem. There

can be a profound sense of guilt for not having lived up to their Ideal. Ultimately, these individuals can go into a chronic state of depression, which can severely undermine both their mental and physical health. Their achievements say they should be happy, but they are very unhappy.

Measuring by Actual[1] always leads to a sense of success and happiness.
When we measure our achievements (Actual[2]) against where we've come from (Actual[1]), we always have a sense of progress. Why is that? Because, unlike the Ideal, the starting point that we call Actual[1] is real. It actually exists. We were there; we know what it felt like. The Ideal exists only in our imagination. People who measure by the Ideal live in a fantasy world. No one else can know or understand what they are using for their measurement. But Actual[1] exists in the real world. It exists in time and in space, and, most important, it can be verified by other people.

Individuals who measure their achievements by Actual[1] always have a sense of success. And with every new success comes a greater sense of satisfaction. There's an overall experience of increasing capability and confidence. With these also comes high self-esteem. There's a profound enjoyment of every experience in life. With each new success, there is a heightened sense of optimism because the future has always turned out to be better than the past.

All the things we measure in our lives.
Here is a list of just a few of the things we measure in our lives:
- Physical appearance
- Health and vitality
- Intelligence
- Talents of every kind
- Wealth
- Popularity
- Status in society
- Education
- Possessions
- Sexuality
- Youthfulness and aging
- Relationships

Our entire consciousness.
In each area, we are continually creating powerful ideals, and from these ideals, we continually establish goals for progress

and self-improvement. Our entire consciousness is made up of our aspirations to become better human beings based on our ideals — not just in these areas, but in countless others as well.

Imagine, then, the enormous pain there must be for the individual who measures his or her achievements by the Ideal attached to each of these areas. In every area of measurement, he or she feels like a failure — in spite of the fact the person may actually be extraordinarily beautiful, intelligent, talented, successful, and surrounded by advantages and privileges.

Who achieves more: A's or B's?
This question goes to the crux of the matter. It helps to explain why the A's — those individuals who measure their achievements against the Ideal — continue to do so, even though it causes them so much unhappiness. You see, the "A" person believes that all the feelings of failure and frustration are simply the price to be paid for being such a high achiever. Yes, they are unhappy, but it keeps them going, it keeps them from stagnating, it keeps them from becoming complacent.

But look at the B's — those who measure their achievements against Actual[1]. Are they not also high achievers? Are there not just as many B's who are high achievers? The truth of the matter about human achievement is that it doesn't make any difference whether you are an A or a B. Both can be equally high achievers. But it makes all the difference in the world to whether you are going to be happy or not. The B's are the only achievers who actually experience the happiness of achievement.

The two zones of human life.
There is no one who is a total A or a total B. All of us have a mixture of the two in our thinking. As children, we learn to measure ourselves predominantly by either the Ideal or by Actual[1]. This can happen for a variety of reasons. For example, a child whose parents measure

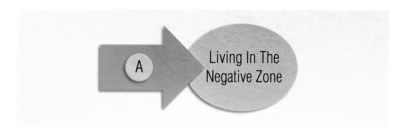

themselves by the Ideal is also likely to do this. There are religions, as well as school systems, that put enormous emphasis on measuring by the Ideal. There are whole national cultures that are preoccupied with the Ideal, where people are expected to feel guilty when they fail to achieve perfection.

Living in The Negative Zone.

A child who grows to adulthood in these kinds of environments — without any countervailing influence — is highly likely to become an A. He or she will live a whole lifetime, then, in what is called "The Negative Zone." Even though there may be moments of happiness throughout this person's life, the overriding experience will always be a negative one marked by the guilt of failing to achieve perfection.

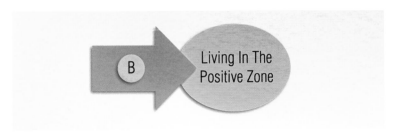

Living in The Positive Zone.
Individuals who measure themselves by Actual[1] do not lead perfect lives. But they do lead lives of continual progress. Even though they experience momentary periods of unhappiness throughout their lives, their overriding experience is one of success and happiness. They live in "The Positive Zone."

Change of thinking and habits.
If you are an A, can you become a B? If you have spent most of your life in The Negative Zone, can you move to The Positive Zone? The answer to both questions is "yes"; however, it requires a profound change in thoughts and habits. You must realize the importance of measuring yourself by your Actual[1] and not by the Ideal. Make this a daily thought. On the following pages are 12 life strategies that, as they become habits of action, will bring you increasingly into The Positive Zone.

The 12 Strategies

Strategy 1

Take a whole day for yourself to write your lifetime ideals, which, when you're finished, should fit on one sheet of paper. Make sure your goals are larger than you are; that is, that they're about improving the world. The happiest people are those who see their lifetime as a positive and creative contribution to the human race. On the other hand, the unhappiest people are those whose ideals only concern themselves. Ask yourself this question: "In what ways do I want the world to be a better place for my having been here?" Use this as the basis for clarifying your ideals.

Strategy 2

Increase your ability to establish and achieve goals — and to acknowledge and celebrate progress.

Most people are unconscious goal setters. They don't clearly identify what their goals are, and they don't write them down. Furthermore, they don't give themselves deadlines. Because of this, it's difficult for them to recognize their achievements. There are two key things to do here. First, write your goals down, making sure that they are specific and measurable, and give yourself deadlines for achieving them. Second, review your progress on a daily basis and continually celebrate your progress. When you have achieved your goals, acknowledge your success and celebrate.

Strategy 3

Increase the daily time focused on your Unique Ability® — and create a Unique Ability® Team.

You have a Unique Ability. It lies in a small group of activities that you are passionate about and where you have a superior skill that provides you and others with a great deal of energy. Another key feature of these Unique Ability activities is that you never stop improving your ability. It is important to focus your time more and more on these activities, and delegate all non-Unique Ability activities to a team of other individuals whose own Unique Abilities lie in doing these. The more you free yourself up in this way, the more you will live in The Positive Zone.

Strategy 4

Increase your ability to "be present" on a daily basis in all life situations.

People who spend most of their time in The Negative Zone live either in the past, where they feel guilty about their failures, or in the future, where they dread more frustration. They almost never live in the present. They're always obsessed with the Ideal, with achieving perfection. As a result, "real life" for them always lies ahead. It's never right now. Take time each day to appreciate being "here." Don't · think about the past. Don't worry about the future. Since you're always making progress, always measuring by Actual1, you can afford the luxury of just enjoying each experience as it happens.

Strategy 5

Increase the integration of all aspects of both your personal and professional life.

People in The Negative Zone have a tendency to "compartmentalize" their lives. There's no integrity between one part of their life and another. They say one thing, but do another. This leads to a life that is false, shallow, and hollow. These people feel increasingly isolated because they don't want anyone to see who they actually are. Therefore, you should continually strive for consistency throughout your life, bringing your thoughts into alignment with your words, and your words into alignment with your actions. This will give you a growing sense of internal strength and serenity.

Strategy 6

Increase your ability to "create value" in all life situations.

Value creation consists of three different kinds of activities: leadership, where you provide other people with direction; relationship, where you provide them with confidence; and creativity, where you provide others with new capabilities. In all places and at all times, these three activities do the most good and are the most highly acclaimed and rewarded. In all of your relationships — both public and private — approach each day and each situation by asking yourself how you're going to provide others with greater direction, confidence, and capability.

Being "referable" means that the best people say the best things about you and your organization. It means that everyone wants everybody else to know good things about you. In order to increase your referability, you have to strengthen the four crucial Referability Habits™:
• Show up on time.
• Do what you say.
• Finish what you start.
• Say please and thank you.

Only people who practice these habits on a daily basis get referred. This is true at all times, in all places. All referability starts here.

Strategy 8

Increase your ability to transform all obstacles into creative solutions.

For many people, an "obstacle" means a dead end. There's no use trying; you can't go any further. But for creative people — especially those who live in The Positive Zone — an obstacle is simply raw material for creating innovative solutions. The moment your mind fixes on an ideal and then sets a goal, it also alerts you to all the things that can prevent you from reaching that goal. These are the obstacles. It's simply your brain's way of telling you: "In order to get to this goal, these are the things that you will need to transform and change." The obstacles are simply raw material.

Strategy 9

Increase your ability to differentiate yourself — both personally and organizationally.

It's one thing to be good at what you do, but another to have other people know how good you are. Many people spend their whole lives focusing on self-improvement, without giving any thought to self-differentiation. To differentiate yourself means to bring yourself uniquely to the attention of the people who can most utilize, appreciate, and reward your abilities. This requires that who you are and what you do be seen as new, different, and better. Right now, there are thousands of people who are looking for you. Make sure you present yourself in a way that they can find you.

Strategy 10

Increase your ability to achieve higher levels of personal and organizational productivity.

The vast majority of people today still operate according to a "bureaucratic time system" — dividing their life rigidly between 9-to-5 workdays and weekends. This system leads to a low level of productivity. The most creative people, however, operate according to The Entrepreneurial Time System®, which is divided into Free, Focus, and Buffer Days. Free Days™ are for rejuvenation, Focus Days™ are for productivity, and Buffer Days™ are for preparation. When an organization enables its people to operate according to this entrepreneurial system, their productivity soars.

Strategy 11

Bureaucracy is based on the principle that human beings are essentially non-learning and non-creative. In other words, it treats people as unthinking machinery. The result is predictable: After only a short period in a bureaucracy, most people stop learning and stop creating. They get tangled in bureaucratic values, conflicts, and dependencies, thus spending their entire lives in The Negative Zone. The opposite of bureaucracy is entrepreneurism, the lifelong activity of creating new value for other human beings. To avoid bureaucracy, think and act like an entrepreneur.

Strategy 12

Increase your ability to take advantage of entrepreneurial opportunities in the global economy.

The world favors entrepreneurs, those who are continually creating value — products, services, and experiences that are new, better, and different. The crucial breakthroughs in the entrepreneurial transformation of the world over the past 25 years have been the microchip, the personal computer, and, now, the Internet. Millions of entrepreneurially-minded people now have the ability to communicate and create with each other, bypassing bureaucratic controls. This is an extraordinary period in human history. Take advantage of it.

A lifetime of constantly increasing positive experiences.
There is no perfection in The Positive Zone, only increased progress on an ongoing basis. Instead of trying to reach the Ideal, people who live in The Positive Zone continually work to bring more of the spirit and practicality of the 12 strategies into their daily lives. The reward for this effort is an increasing sense of success, satisfaction, and overall happiness. On the other hand, those who pursue the Ideal and use it to measure their performance are doomed to a lifetime of unhappiness.

It's a simple thing to escape from this trap. Begin measuring all your achievements by Actual[1], then increase the positive quality of each day's experience by implementing the 12 strategies.

Strategic Coach®: A lifetime school for learning to live more fully in The Positive Zone.
These concepts of avoiding The Gap and living in The Positive Zone are part of the Strategic Coach® Program, a lifetime focusing and learning program for highly successful entrepreneurs.

Increased value creation.
Strategic Coach is designed to assist those individuals who have already proven themselves as entrepreneurs to lead happier and more productive lives — and to increase the value they create for all the people in their lives and communities.

The Program itself consists of an ongoing series of full-day workshops at 90-day intervals, during which the participants clarify their lifetime ideals and transform them into a series of three-year, three-month, weekly, and daily goals.

Simplicity, balance, and focus.
The overall impact of this process is that entrepreneurs are able to simplify their work, achieve greater balance between their business and personal lives, and create a support team that enables them to focus entirely on their own Unique Ability. They have an ever-increasing sense of happiness from their participation in the global economy that will define the 21st century.

Support teams and families.
In addition to the main program for entrepreneurs,
Strategic Coach also offers additional conferences and
workshops for members of the entrepreneur's support
team and for members of his or her family.

Knowledge Products.
This presentation of The Gap concept is one of a growing
list of Knowledge Products offered by Strategic Coach.
All are designed to help individuals and groups to live
and work increasingly in The Positive Zone.

Further information.
For further information on Strategic Coach programs and
Knowledge Products, phone **416.531.7399** or **1.800.387.3206**.
Or visit us online at *www.strategiccoach.com*.